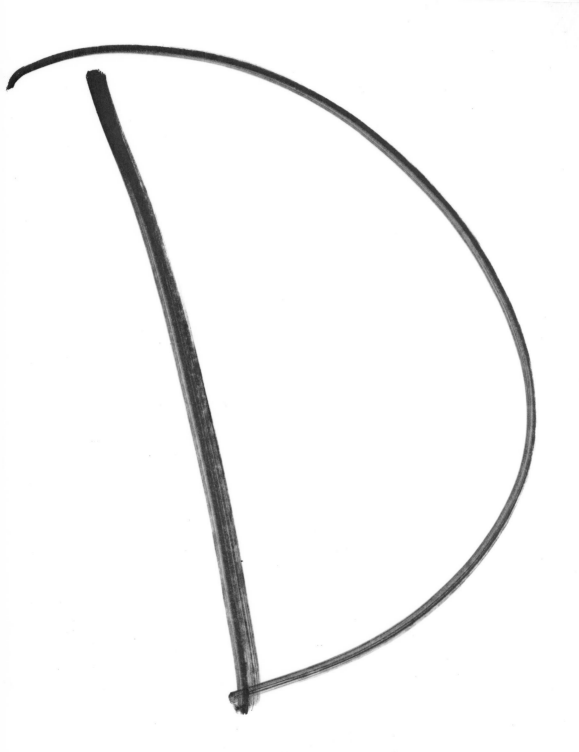

ON THE MAP

GERMANY

Titles in this Series:

Canada	Japan
China	Mexico
Egypt	Russia
France	Spain
Germany	U.S.A.
Italy	West Indies

Editor: Marian L. Edwards
Design: M&M partnership
Electronic production: Scott Melcer
Photographs: ZEFA except
   Chris Fairclough (18)
Map artwork: Raymond Turvey
Cover photo: Munich

Library of Congress Cataloging-in-Publication Data

Flint, David, 1946–
    Germany / David Flint
      p.   cm. — (On the map)
    Includes bibliographical references and index.
    Summary: An illustrated introduction to the geography, people,
family life, food, schools, industry, and famous landmarks of
Germany.
    ISBN 0–8114–3418–4
    1. Germany — Juvenile literature.   [1. Germany.]   I. Title.
II. Series.
DD17.F55 1994
943–dc20   93–631
                                                                 CIP
                                                                 AC

Printed and bound in the United States.
  2 3 4 5 6 7 8 9 0 VH 98 97 96 95

GERMANY

David Flint

RSVP

RAINTREE STECK-VAUGHN
P U B L I S H E R S
The Steck-Vaughn Company

Austin, Texas

Contents

The Zugspitze, the highest mountain in Germany, has a weather station and is a popular tourist spot.

Rossenbach is typical of many picturesq German villages where buildings date fr the 16th century.

Frankfurt is an impressive mixture of old and new buildings.

Neuschwanstein castle was built by Ludwig II of Bavaria in the 19th century

At the Heart of Europe

Germany is one of the largest countries in Europe. It is in the middle of the continent. Germany shares borders with nine other countries. It has Poland and the Czech Republic to the east. France, Belgium, Luxembourg, and the Netherlands are to the west. To the south, Germany has borders with Switzerland and Austria. To the north is Denmark.

Germany also has a coastline on the North Sea in the northwest. In the northeast, its coastline meets the Baltic Sea. Just off the northwest coast is a cluster of tiny islands.

In the north, the weather is mild and wet in the summer. Winters are cool. In the south, summers are hot, short, and sunny. Winters are cold, with ice and snow. Winter ice forms on many of the rivers in the east and southeast. This can slow up or even stop the flow of river traffic.

Throughout the country, summer is the wettest season of the year. Much of the summer rain falls during severe thunderstorms. These heavy storms can cause sudden floods. Sometimes the floods do a great deal of damage.

Mountains, Forests, and Coasts

Germany has a variety of landscapes. High plains, hills, and thick forests cover the central part of the country. In some places, the forests seem endless.

In the south, the Bavarian Alps form the border between Germany and Austria. These high mountains tower over the surrounding plains. Bright, fast-flowing streams in the deep valleys cut through the mountains on their way to the faraway sea. In some places, castles and tiny mountain villages nestle along the banks of the streams. Some of the castles are centuries old.

In the southwest is the Black Forest. It is the country's largest wooded area. The Black Forest gets its name from the spruce and dark fir trees that grow there. It is a region rich in German legend and folklore. Many fairy tales are set in this forest.

The north coast is lapped by the North Sea in the west, and the Baltic Sea in the east. Both coasts have long, sandy beaches. The coastal areas are milder than the inland areas. Summers are usually sunny, but the seas stay very cold. The cold water does not stop the Germans who flock to beaches to lie in the summer sun. Some even swim in the chilly waters.

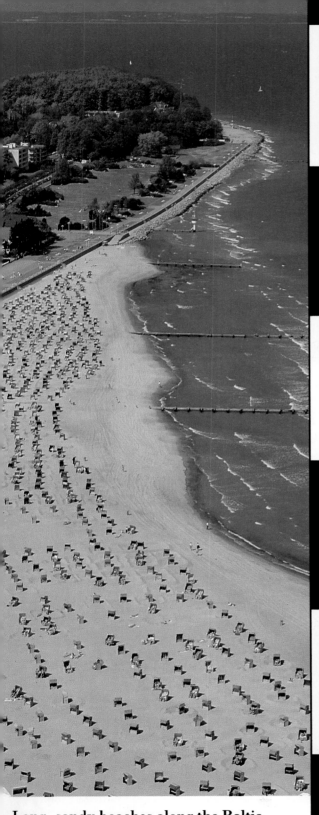

High mountain peaks like the Zugspitze make southern Germany a popular skiing area.

Long, sandy beaches along the Baltic coast are crowded in summer despite the cool temperature of the sea.

The vast Black Forest stretches across much of southern Germany. It is a favorite place for tourists.

The important port of Hamburg has grown up where the Elbe River meets the North Sea. Ships from around the world come to this port.

The Rhine River at Düsseldorf with factories, offices, highways, and modern hotels.

At the River

Three large rivers flow through Germany. The longest is the Rhine River. It travels northward from Switzerland, through a valley between the Black Forest and the Vosges Mountains. Then it bends westward through the Netherlands and on to the North Sea. The Rhine River is one of the world's greatest commercial waterways.

The Elbe is the second-longest river in Germany. It flows from the Czech Republic through the Harz Mountains. From the Harz Mountains it travels on to the North Sea. At the mouth of the Elbe is the city of Hamburg. This city is Germany's busiest port. Hamburg's industries center around shipping and shipbuilding. The deep waters of the Elbe River allow the world's largest ships to get in and out of Hamburg.

The Danube River rises in southern Germany. It flows eastward through Austria. From Austria, the Danube turns southward on its way to the Black Sea. The Danube carries many industrial products to other European countries.

Germany has many other rivers. A system of canals connects the major rivers and waterways.

Day and night, Berlin, the capital of Germany, is a bustling city.
Many companies have their headquarters here where highways meet.

Alexanderplatz in the eastern part of
Berlin. Cars are banned and trains
shuttle people around the city.

When the Berlin Wall was torn down i
1989, many people collected their ow
souvenirs.

Berlin

About 78 million people live in Germany. Most live in large towns and cities. A few people still prefer to live in villages in the countryside.

Berlin, in northeast Germany, is the capital and largest city. Over 3 million people live there. Berlin is the center of government, international trade, and banking. It is also known as Germany's most important spot for cultural activities.

For many years, Germany was divided into two countries—East Germany and West Germany. Berlin, like Germany, was also divided into East Berlin and West Berlin. This division lasted for about forty years. Then in 1989, the communist government in East Germany fell apart. The wall that had been built across Berlin was joyfully torn down. The two countries reunited, and Germany became one nation again. Berlin once more became the capital city of a unified Germany.

Today Berlin is a modern city of skyscrapers and highways. The city's industries produce everything from cars to radios. Stores and shops are well stocked with all kinds of goods. Throughout the city people stroll or sunbathe in parks. Along the wide avenues are restaurants and outdoor cafes.

Fuel for many power stations comes from large strip mines. Coal is removed from the Earth's surface.

Coal from deep mines, like this one in the Ruhr area, provides the fuel for half of Germany's electricity.

Some of Germany's electricity comes from hydroelectric power stations like this one in Schleswig-Holstein.

Power

Coal is an important fuel for industry. Germany has large amounts of coal under the ground. It is found mostly in the Ruhr River valley. Factories were built in the Ruhr valley near the rich coalfields. The coal provides fuel for power stations making electricity. The electricity is used to run homes, shops, offices, farms, and factories.

Germany needs a lot of fuel for its many factories and industries. Its large deposits of coal are not enough. In addition to coal, Germany uses other sources of fuel. It imports oil and natural gas. The oil comes mainly from Saudi Arabia. Natural gas is from the Netherlands.

Coal, oil, and natural gas power stations all pollute the air with smoke. This has become a major problem for Germany. In some parts of the country, swift-flowing rivers make electricity without polluting the air. Electricity made from flowing water is called water power, or hydroelectric power. Water power is one way to help solve the problem of pollution. It is also much cheaper than coal, oil, and natural gas. German scientists continue to look for other pollution-free ways of making electricity.

Families and Food

Food is an important part of German family life. The German people like good food and plenty of it. Family members try to eat most meals together. Mealtime is when they talk about events of the day.

Breakfast is eaten early, before parents go to work and children go to school. It usually consists of bread, rolls, cheese, butter, and jam. Bread is a part of every meal. Over 200 kinds of bread can be found in Germany.

Lunch, the main meal of the day, is eaten around noon or one o'clock. There is usually meat with potatoes and vegetables. Pork is the most popular meat, followed by beef and veal. Vegetables such as beets, onions, carrots, and turnips are eaten in large quantities. Cabbage is also a favorite vegetable. Germans enjoy many different kinds of fish.

In the evening, families eat a light meal. Most often it is bread, cheese, sausage, and salad. Fancy pastries are a special weekend treat.

In the past, most meals were eaten at home. Today, more and more families choose to eat some meals out. Towns and cities have a wide variety of German and foreign restaurants.

Breakfast is an important meal for the whole family. People choose from fruit juices, rolls, cereal, boiled eggs, and cheese.

For lunch, families enjoy a meat dish with potatoes and cooked vegetables.

Children going to school carry books, papers, and sandwiches in their knapsacks.

Creative art classes are an important part of school life.

Going to School

All children in Germany go to school when they are six years old. They go to a four-year elementary school. Some children start kindergarten soon after the age of three.

After elementary school, children can choose from secondary school, middle school, or grammar school. Whatever they choose, children must stay in school until they are at least fourteen years old.

Each state in Germany runs its own schools. Richer states have more money to spend on their schools. But the majority of schools in Germany are known to offer quality education.

The school day starts at eight o'clock in the morning and ends around one o'clock in the afternoon. During the summer months, school starts a little earlier. In most parts of the country, there are also classes on Saturday mornings. Children take sandwiches to school to eat at the midmorning break. They go home for a hot lunch at midday, after school is out.

Many German students continue their education. This is especially true for those who go to secondary schools. They have more than sixty universities and colleges to choose from.

Barges, like this one near Frankfurt, carry heavy industrial goods like coal, steel, and oil.

Trains are fast and frequent in Germany. Platform signs give travel the information they need.

Airports are important in a big country like Germany, where the main towns are far apart.

Germany began to build highways in the 1930s. Modern roads now link all the main areas of the country.

Getting Around

Travel in and around Germany is fast and convenient. Cars are the most popular way to get around. Wide, modern highways, called autobahns, keep the traffic moving smoothly. The autobahn is the longest and busiest highway system in Europe. It links all major industrial centers. It is also one of the fastest highway systems in the world.

Train travel is easy and cheap. High speed Trans-Europe Express (TEE) trains connect German cities with other European cities. These trains provide quick and comfortable service. All of the cars are first-class and have telephones. Germany's railroad system is one of the best in the world.

Airline travel is popular with business people and vacationers. Lufthansa, the country's national airline, has its own train service. These trains carry airline passengers between main airports and nearby cities. Each day planes leave Germany for major cities in other countries.

In towns, people can get around by car, bus, streetcar, or motorcycle. Big cities like Munich, Hamburg, and Berlin have trains that run on a raised track and underground trains. People use them to get around the cities quickly.

On the Farm

More than half of the land in Germany is used for farming. Much of this is dairy farming. The rest of the land is used for raising livestock and growing crops. In the northern part of the country, grass, wheat, and sugar beets grow very well. These crops are fed to cattle, which provide milk, cheese, and meat. In the south, corn is grown to feed the animals.

Potatoes are one of Germany's main crops. Farmers grow enough potatoes to feed all the people in the country. Grains such as oats, rye, and barley are grown in large quantities. In addition, farmers grow fruits and vegetables such as apples, onions, and cabbage. Still, Germany must import more food from other parts of the world.

Farmers raise cattle, sheep, and chickens. But pigs are the number one farm animal. They outnumber all other farm animals in Germany. Germans like to eat wurst, a sausage made from pork, so pig farming is very important all over the country.

Wine has been made in Germany for more than 1,500 years. The grapes grow well on the sunny slopes of the river valleys. Much of Germany's high quality wine is shipped to the United States and other countries.

tra workers help harvest the grapes
ich are used to make wine.

Pigs are raised on large modern farms
like this one in the south.

winter, many farmers keep their cattle indoors where it is warm and dry.

Engineers make a safety check. The German chemical industry employs more than 600,000 people.

Many people go to work in offices like the Berlin Congress Center. Getting to work by car or train is easy.

Shopping centers with offices above are air-conditioned and centrally heated.

Modern industries like electronics provide jobs for skilled workers.

Work

Parts of Germany are experiencing some unemployment, but most people have jobs. The majority of Germans work in stores, offices, and factories. The workday starts between seven and eight o'clock in the morning and ends between five and six o'clock in the evening.

Germany is an industrial giant. This is due partly to its hardworking people. Factories and research centers produce a wide variety of products. German companies have a reputation for making very high quality, reliable goods. Cars, vacuum cleaners, and washing machines are just a few.

Companies also make goods requiring a lot of skill, such as binoculars and fine china. In addition, Germans are known for making delicate tools and instruments, such as electronic equipment.

Today, German industries are among the most successful in Europe. They have given the Germans a high standard of living.

Since the country reunited in 1990, companies in western Germany have started to update factories in the east. This will increase production and the amount of goods Germany exports.

Leisure Time

Playing sports and exercising are very popular in Germany. They are fun to do and healthful. Even in cities, there are fitness trails in the parks and woods. People can jog, run, or walk the trails. Most towns have athletic clubs and centers for gymnastics. Many are free and have the latest equipment.

In winter the mountains in the south offer good skiing and other winter sports. In summer, lakes and rivers provide sailing, surfing, and swimming. Many people go to North Sea resorts and to the islands off the coast.

Soccer is the most popular sport in Germany—with both players and fans. There are thousands of soccer teams across the country. When at home, people like to watch television, read, or play computer games. Many also enjoy gardening.

Festivals are a big part of German life. They are held all over the country. Many festivals are celebrated with parades, brass bands, and colorful costumes. Some places hold gymnastic and sports festivals. These include contests and activities for children of all ages. Each fall more than five million people attend Oktoberfest. The city of Munich is known for this festival where people eat, drink, and enjoy music.

During the summer people enjoy sitting at outdoor cafes in cities like Berlin.

On the slopes east of Regensburg, students get last minute instructions.

Every autumn, thousands of people flock to Munich for the Oktoberfest.

Famous Landmarks

The valley of the Rhine River in autumn—one of Germany's most important wine producing regions.

The Poseidon Building in Frankfurt is an impressive example of modern German architecture.

The Reichstag in Berlin is the home of the German parliament.

Meissen, in the east on the Elbe River, is famous for fine china.

Beethoven's house in Bonn is now a museum devoted to the composer.

The Brandenburg Gate in Berlin, closed for many years, is again one of the busiest junctions in Europe.

The Rhine River near the Lorelei, where, according to legend, a singing maiden lured barges onto the rock.

Facts and Figures

Germany—the Land and People

Population:	about 78 million
Area:	about 138,000 sq. mi.
Length north-south: east-west:	about 550 mi. about 400 mi.
Capital city: population:	Berlin about 3 million
Language:	German
Religion:	Protestant and Roman Catholic, but many other religions practiced
School hours:	7:30–8:00 A.M. until 1:00–1:30 P.M. Monday to Friday 10:00 A.M. until 12:00 noon Saturdays
Business hours:	8:00 A.M. until 6:00 P.M. (1–2 hours for lunch)
Money:	Deutsche mark (DM)

What Happened When

Date	Event
1945	World War II ended—Berlin and Germany were divided.
1948	Berlin airlift—the road linking West Germany and West Berlin is closed by communist East Germany, so West Berlin supplied with food and coal by planes from the U.S., France, and Great Britain.
1955	West Germany became an independent nation.
1958	Treaties signed setting up the European Economic Community—West Germany was a founding member.
1961	Wall built across Berlin by East Germany to stop people leaving the East for the West.
1989	Communist power in East Germany collapsed and the Berlin Wall was demolished.
1990	Elections held which resulted in the reunification of East and West Germany as one nation.

Landmarks

Highest mountain:	Zugspitze Mountain 9,721 ft.
Longest river:	Rhine River 820 mi.
Largest lake:	Constance 210 sq. mi.

Average Temperatures in Fahrenheit

Location	January	June
Berlin (east)	27°F	68°F
Munich (south)	25°F	69°F
Hamburg (north and west)	32°F	63°F

Further Reading

Bradley, John and Catherine. *Germany: The Reunification of a Nation.* Watts, New York, 1991.

Haskins, Jim. *Count Your Way Through Germany.* Carolrhoda, Minneapolis, MN, 1990.

Phillpotts, Beatrice. *Germany.* People and Places Series. Silver Burdett, Englewood Cliffs, 1989.

Schloredt, Valeria. *West Germany: the Land and Its People.* Silver Burdett, Englewood Cliffs, 1988.

Stewart, Gail B. *Germany.* Macmillan Children's Group, New York, 1990.

Audio-Visuals

Audio Cassettes

Mahoney, Judy. *Teach Me German.* Teach Me Tapes, Inc., Minneapolis, MN, 1985

Index